Usborne
Zoo
matching Games

Illustrated by Emily Emerson
Designed by Krysia Ellis
Written by Kate Nolan

Contents

Look through the cards, and
match each one to an animal in
this book to find out its name
and a fun fact about it.

Tiger

Tigers are the biggest cats on Earth. Their stripes help them to stay hidden when they're hunting in the wild.

Squirrel monkey

Speedy squirrel monkeys leap through the treetops, using their long, thick tails for balance.

Scarlet macaw

Scarlet macaws are very clever — some of them even learn to say human words by copying what they hear.

Orangutan

This peaceful ape's arms are longer than its legs, helping it to climb among the branches.

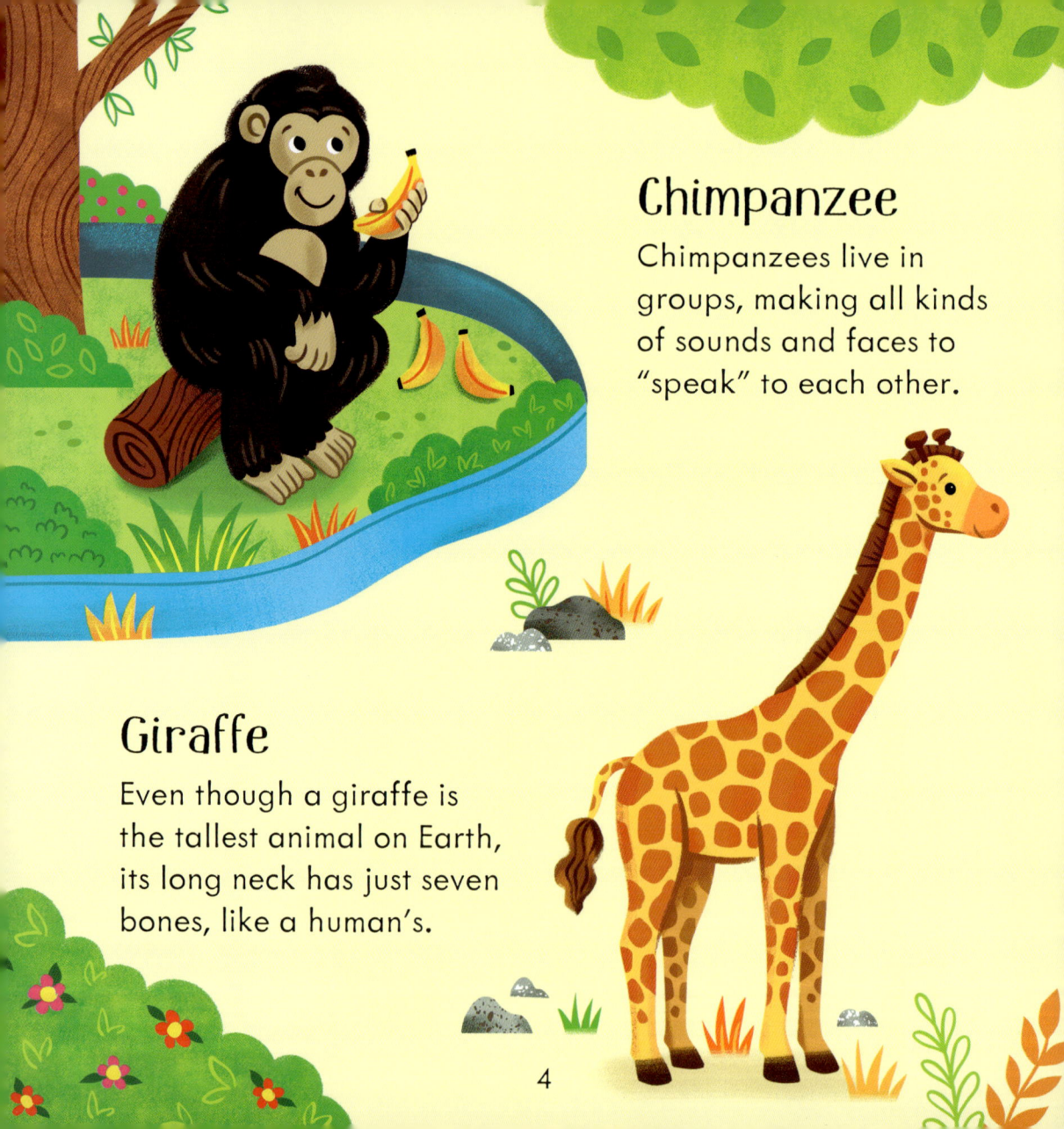

Chimpanzee

Chimpanzees live in groups, making all kinds of sounds and faces to "speak" to each other.

Giraffe

Even though a giraffe is the tallest animal on Earth, its long neck has just seven bones, like a human's.

4

Rhinoceros

Huge and hefty, a rhino can weigh more than a car. Its full name means "nose horn."

Gorilla

These gentle giants are about as tall as humans, but up to ten times stronger.

Toucan

A toucan's big, bright beak has a sharp edge for peeling rainforest fruits to eat.

Ring-tailed lemur

Male lemurs give off a very strong smell — the top lemur in a group is the one with the stinkiest tail!

Sloth

Slow-moving sloths spend most of their time hanging in the treetops, only coming down about once a week.

Rainbow lorikeet

This bird loves fruit and other sweet treats. Its long, hairy tongue lets it eat pollen and nectar from flowers.

Elephant

Stomp, stomp, stomp! Enormous elephants are the biggest land animals on the planet.

Flamingo

Flamingos like to stand on one leg in shallow water, dipping down to find food in the mud at the bottom.

Camel

Camels store fat in their humps for energy, so they can go for days without eating or drinking.

Cheetah

The speediest animals on land, long-legged cheetahs can run faster than a car over short distances.

Reticulated python

One of the biggest snakes on the planet, this python can grow longer than a giraffe is tall.

Crocodile

Some crocodiles have more than 100 sharp, pointed teeth in their snapping jaws.

Chameleon

A chameleon's skin changes when it's scared, or excited, or when it's too warm or too cold.

King cobra

This venomous snake rears up and flares its scaly neck-flaps when it feels frightened.

Zebra

No two zebras have the same pattern of stripes – they are as different as human fingerprints.

Mandrill

Male mandrills stand out in a crowd thanks to their bright faces and blue-and-purple bottoms!

Lion

A male lion has a shaggy mane and a thunderous roar that can be heard from miles away.

Meerkat

These little animals often stand up on their back legs near their burrows, keeping a lookout.

Poison dart frog

No longer than your little finger, these frogs are tiny but deadly – their bright skin is toxic.

Terrapin

These little turtles sunbathe on land to warm up, but they're also strong swimmers.

Axolotl

An axolotl spends its whole life underwater, breathing through the frilly gills on its neck.

Fire salamander

Despite its name, a fire salamander likes to hide in cool, damp places to keep its skin moist.

Tamarin

These tiny monkeys
chirp and whistle to
each other as they
leap lightly from
branch to branch.

Giant panda

A giant panda is only the
size of a pet hamster when
it's born, but it grows to be
taller than an adult human.

Snow leopard

A silvery snow leopard
stays warm on winter
days by wrapping its
fluffy tail around its
body like a scarf.

Red panda

Shy red pandas spend
their days snoozing
high in the treetops,
only waking up as
night falls.

Jewel beetle

This bright beetle gets its name from its shiny, metallic shell. Its delicate wings are folded safely underneath.

Praying mantis

These bugs stand perfectly still, blending in with leaves and twigs, as they wait to pounce on smaller insects.

Butterfly

There are more than 17,000 different kinds of butterflies in the world – they live on every continent except Antarctica.

Tarantula

These spiders are huge and hairy, but harmless to humans – they only eat smaller animals.

How to play zoo match-up

A memory matching game for 2–4 players

1. Each player takes a board:

2. Mix up the cards and lay them all out, face down.

3. Take turns to choose a card and turn it over.

4. If you turn over a card that matches a picture on your board, put the card on top.

It's a rhino. Yes, I need this one!

5. If you don't need the card, put it back where you found it, face down. Then it's the next player's turn.

A panda... that's not on my board.

6. You win by being the first to fill your board.

Top tip: when another player turns over a card you need, remember where it is so you can pick it up on your next turn.

How to play zoo bingo

A matching game for 2–5 players

1. One person mixes up all the cards. That person is the caller.
Everyone else takes a board:

2. The caller picks up the top card and describes what's on it
to the others. Start off with simple details, like this:

It's a bird with
bright feathers.

(If there aren't enough players to have a caller,
players can take turns to say what's on the cards.)

3. If the card matches a picture on someone's board, that player takes it and puts it down on top of the picture.

Is it this one?

No, its beak is red.

What about this one?

Yes!

4. If no one needs the card, put it at the bottom of the pile.

5. Keep going until one player's board is complete. That player is the winner, and has to shout "Bingo!"

It's orange, with black stripes.

Yes, I've got that one too! Bingo!

Top tip: once you're more familiar with the pictures, you could try saying their names, or even using facts from this book to describe them:

Reticulated python

The longest snake on Earth

Index